"Sister Maria Reilly's reflections on [the perspective of age and wisdom sights on an experience each of us is racing or will face. In poetic and simple language, this book becomes a source of life for the reader. The perspective of age provides unique eyes to appreciate the blessings that can come from growing old. Maria Reilly offers us this gift."

Thomas J. Murphy
Archbishop of Seattle

"Clearly, we have here a deeply spiritual woman who has indeed asked vital questions about life's fundamental meaning, and she provides excellent guidance for others asking the same kinds of questions. Blending the multifaceted experiences of her own long life with the timeless (ageless?) insights of Scripture, Sr. Maria has given us perhaps the greatest gift and most worthy legacy possible: the wisdom of one who has been where all of us, *Deo volente*, will one day find ourselves.

"The book can be read profitably by those of any age. In fact I am increasingly convinced that this is exactly the kind of information that must be conveyed to people when they are younger. Some of her insights can be of real value to younger people as they begin to face the reality of their own (and their parents') aging."

Stephen Sapp, Ph.D.
Author, *Full of Years: Aging and the Elderly in the Bible*

"Sister Maria Reilly's faith in God works for her as she faces problems of retirement, old age, and death. Her thoughts about death will be especially helpful to the elderly."

Ruth Morrison, Dawn Radtke
Authors, *Aging with Joy*

"Maria Reilly has given us a string of pearls written in her old age. I love her way of discovering herself and her world at a time when many elderly are wondering about the meaning of life and the preciousness of old age. She has learned that old age is the best time of our life to grow into a fulfilled personality."

Louis J. Putz, C.S.C.
Founder of Forever Learning and Harvest House

"I was moved by *Now That I Am Old*, grateful that such a rich and useful resource is available. Both Sister Maria's style and the plan of the book—brief, open-ended segments—lend themselves to the kind of unhurried reflection she advocates for her readers. The author never sidesteps the less rosy aspects of old age: suffering, feeling forgotten, 'fear of growing grumpy,' regrets, as well as loss of a partner and facing one's own death. But she places them in the context of finally, in late life, having the time to face and work through them. It is this even-handed blend of realism and hopefulness that makes the book so nourishing and useful.

"I would recommend *Now That I Am Old* both to the elderly and to those who work with them, as a way of hearing from one articulate and faithful elderly person what that stage of life is like."

Margot Hover
Duke University Medical Center
Author, *Caring for Yourself When Caring for Others*

"At first glance, the book appears to be only the fruit of four-score years of one Christian's reflections on the mysteries of life. However, the reader soon discovers that this book is an irresistible invitation to engage in the same kind of reflective process. Each of the nearly one hundred single-page essays could lead to days of musing and meditation on the fundamental questions of life. The winter of life ought to give us the leisure to pursue them, and thus to discover that, as the author declares, the mature years can be the best years of all.

"The author deals with issues of particular urgency in one's later years. These range from the demands of divesting oneself of excess baggage and coping with physical diminishment, to the challenges of coping with widowhood and terminal illness.

"The reader will find here no ready-made answers, only a guide to the questions that must be embraced if one wishes to draw full value from the final stages of life on Earth."

Kathryn Kurtz, S.P.

NOW THAT I AM OLD

Meditations on the Meaning of Life

MARIA REILLY, S.P.

TWENTY-THIRD PUBLICATIONS
Mystic, Connecticut 06355

Twenty-Third Publications
185 Willow Street
P.O. Box 180
Mystic, CT 06355
(203) 536-2611
800-321-0411

ISBN 0-89622-559-3
Library of Congress Catalog Card Number 92-63179
Printed in the U.S.A.

Preface

As far back as I can remember, I have wrestled with questions that add up to one overriding question: What is life all about? This question began to tease me when I was only five years old and is yet with me decades later. To me, even now when I am almost ninety years old, it is a query that keeps my mind alert and open to reality.

The very fact that I have reached a mature age assures me both impunity and the leisure time for pondering the fundamental puzzle our humanity poses: the meaning of life.

I find it exciting to wrestle with this question, since it must be considered in every conscious moral choice.

I still find myself puzzling over very basic questions: Who am I? What is life all about?

What should fill my days now that my professional careers have wound down and retirement provides me leisure hours I could only dream of during decades of daily work obligations?

What am I to make of this piece of life when physical weakness often dictates a slowed-down pace and sometimes clouds my spiritual vision? If I could read our Creator's mind, what would I find is the purpose of these latter years? What should I be making of them?

The thoughts expressed in this small book are the fruit of my own reflections about life and particularly about the retirement years.

Many of the ideas grew directly out of my several years as Director of Retirement for my own Providence community of religious women, and then from my fourteen years experience as a minister to the elderly in a fairly large Seattle parish.

I gained much from the questions presented to me during those nearly two decades of work with the elderly and from the unspoken questions—and answers—written on the faces and in the postures of the wonderful persons I met and called friends.

These pages are directed primarily to those who, like me, have already traveled a long way on life's journey and who, like me, are still struggling with the fundamental human questions that help give life meaning and purpose.

I do not pretend to offer answers, for I am still seeking those, but I have come to believe that the search itself is part of the answer. These reflections offer some ideas, observations, and suggestions that have proved useful to me as I strive to make my retirement years productive and purposeful.

I began recording my ideas simply as a way of clarifying my own thinking about aging and about retirement. Friends and acquaintances with whom I shared some of my reflections urged me to widen the scope of my writing and thus perhaps assist others on the same journey.

This small volume results from their encouragement. I am grateful to them and to all I have met along the way for helping to shape the person I am today. If even one person finds life more meaningful and joyous as a result of this book, my purpose in offering it for publication will have been amply fulfilled.

My special thanks to two members of my religious community without whose encouragement and help I would not have pursued and completed this project: Sister Clare Lentz, S.P. (Spokane, Washington), for encouragement, and Sister Maryann Benoit, S.P. (Great Falls, Montana), for editing the manuscript.

Contents

Preface *v*

PART ONE
Facing the Inevitable: Retirement 1

PART TWO
Questioning 11

PART THREE
I Have Walked with Them 22

PART FOUR
Who Am I Now That I am Old and Retired? 29

PART FIVE
Time to Take Stock 35

PART SIX
The Art of Letting Go 41

PART SEVEN
Travelers on the Way Home 48

PART EIGHT
Those Who Mourn: The Widowed 56

PART NINE
Suffering Can Transform 67

PART TEN
That Five-Letter Word 74

PART ELEVEN
Probing Life's Mystery 84

PART TWELVE
Mary, Post-Resurrection Woman:
Patroness of the Elderly 91

PART THIRTEEN
Walking in Hope and Trust 98

PART FOURTEEN
Epilogue: Then and Now 107

NOW THAT
I AM OLD

PART ONE

Facing the Inevitable: Retirement

Only developed societies have the luxury of a piece of life called "retirement." As improvements in health care have brought more individuals to this point in life, some find themselves uncertain about what to do with new-found spare time. Is there a task appropriate to this part of life?

1. Retirement

Retired. What a strange word. What does it really mean? Life goes on as usual around me. Radio, television, daily papers, and magazines continue to bring me news of the world near and far. By letter and telephone I keep in touch with friends. I continue my lifetime regimen of varied activities, including prayer. Life goes on at its usual pace. Yet I am retired.

This is a hard concept to fathom. For years I have tried to prepare myself for this time of life, and now I find that the preparation time is over and the reality of retirement is here. What's my job now?

2. Unique Task

What is the task of the elderly person during life's later years? If there is a particular task, who is the beneficiary? And I ask several friends the same questions. A woman who had taken a job as a waitress after her husband's health failed responded: "I believe that during these last years of life I should enjoy the things I missed in earlier years. I want to go on tours, meet friends, have time to do the things I enjoy doing."

Another woman said: "I see my life as cementing— holding together family members, children, in-laws, grandchildren. I see my task as an outreach to these and others. I want to be supportive of the life and the activities of our parish. Over and above all this, I want to grow in love of God."

Another mother of a grown family sees her mission in life's later years as "listening to the guidance of the Holy Spirit." She adds, "After that, I do things as they come."

A professor of psychology gave an answer that puzzled me at first. He said simply, "I see my task as making sure I don't get grumpy." His other task, he added, is "growth in nearness to God."

The greatest task of the elderly, another told me, is adaptability: "Learn to adapt to limitations imposed by age and health; adapt to circumstances; adapt to a changing world and culture."

Still another sums up in one word her recipe: "Volunteer." She finds volunteering satisfyingly productive.

What indeed is the right task for the elderly?

3. Retirement Questions

Comments on the aging process and on retirement status are not always upbeat.

Often in their unguarded conversations the elderly voice less positive attitudes in the form of somewhat querulous questions:

"What use am I now that I can no longer do anything?"

"Why do I have to suffer like this?"

"Has God forgotten me?"

"I wish that when I was younger I had known what I now know. Why did I have to learn the hard way?"

4. What Is Life All About?

From the perspective of age and experience, people have to face a basic question: What is the rock-bottom question that leads to understanding the meaning of life?

The real question such people are asking adds up to something like this: "What is life all about? Does life have meaning beyond the immediate experience? What is the meaning of life at this stage? Does life have a goal? What can make living worthwhile when so much has changed for me?"

Indeed, life could seem burdensome and meaningless in the latter years if one measured its value only in terms of full physical vigor, job satisfaction, peer approval and perhaps admiration, unbounded youthful enthusiasm, seemingly limitless possibilities, and a multiplicity of social involvements.

5. Purpose and Goal

For everything there is a season, and the retirement years have their own purpose and possibilities.

I see these years as a time of summing up, of bringing into unity what has gone before, of seeing life's details in relation to the whole.

I see these years as a time of letting go of non-essentials, a time for focusing attention on what lies yet ahead. These years offer a time for finding within myself the reservoir of strength and ingenuity needed to meet new kinds of challenges. This is a time for measuring myself against the ideals of wholeness and maturity by which I have—perhaps unconsciously—judged others.

Perhaps most of all I see these years as a time of gratitude for the conviction I have that a benevolent God not only sustains us in life but also intends for us a life that never ends, a new life beyond this one that will be the answer to the ever-nagging question, "Why am I here? What's it all about?"

6. Is Being Old Also Being Wise?

Commonly, we associate wisdom with age, and for many older adults the wisdom of the ages found in the Bible becomes more precious and more revealing as they find themselves with more time available for reflection.

The Bible traces God's relationship with the works of creation, particularly with the human beings whose gift of intellect can let them realize their magnificent endowments. The unconditional love of God for us gives us our dignity, our worth, our sense of purpose. The scriptural record of this provident love supplies the answer to many questions about life's meaning. God's faithfulness to humankind is a covenant calling for a response of gratitude. It calls also for a sense of responsibility for life's gifts to us.

7. Love, the Meaning of Life

Love is the meaning of life, for the God who has created and who sustains us in life is Love.

Our existence attests to God's provident love. For some of us, it may well be that we understand that truth as if for the first time when we at last enjoy the leisure to reflect on and make sense of our lives.

We have a purpose and the latter years may be the best time for rooting deeply within ourselves an all-pervasive conviction: What is truly good or precious in our lives should speak to us of our favored status as people of a loving God.

We cannot do better than to recall each day that at the end of life we will be examined on love.

The mature years serve their purpose if they ready us for that ultimate goal of life with God forever.

No matter that our steps may be slower and our memories a bit faulty: We all know the power of love, and we can find ways to let God's unconditional love for us be mirrored increasingly in our thinking and in our actions toward those around us.

8. Making Up for Lost Time

Retirement gives us time to grow into our best selves. Retirement lets us make up for time lost earlier to less beneficial pursuits. Freed of pressing obligations, we have the enviable opportunity to explore ways to enrich our lives and possibly to enrich the lives of others as well.

Time need never be long for the individual who sets goals to achieve. Indeed, time will seem too short for the person who, with Robert Frost, has "promises to keep" and "miles to go" before he sleeps.

Viewed as an opportunity, the mature years can be the best years of all.

9. Retired? No, Re-tired

The family car had served us well
for nearly fourteen years.
It carried Mom when Joe was born;
it knew our joys and fears.

The family car had seen the road
of mile on mile for years.
But now its usefulness seemed gone.
We heard the news with tears.

But younger hearts had other plans,
a way to save the car.
The frame is firm, the engine good;
its finish, though, has scars.

A few cosmetics, a little paint,
will make the car look new.
With tires on both front and back
and adjustments not a few.

Re-tired now, our family car
is ready for the road
To bring us here and take us there
and carry many a load.

PART TWO

Questioning

Any new experience fills the mind with questions.
Whether we had anticipated retirement with dread or
with eagerness, we still face the unfamiliar, the untried.
We wonder: What will this be like? Am I ready for this?
At a deeper level, we will sense that deeper questions
beg to be addressed now that time allows reflection.

10. The Mystery of Life

At some point in life, each of us experienced the mystery of life for the first time.

I remember sitting at a table, my chin resting on my folded arms, and looking at my five-year-old reflection in a mirror. I looked, looked, and looked. I was already beginning to experience the mysteriousness of life and was puzzled.

I looked into my reflected eyes, seeking an answer. I wanted to know who was inside there, behind those eyes. I wanted to know myself. I wanted to know what was going on.

At five, one does not formulate thoughts into words, so I finally abandoned the mirror and continued living the wonderful mystery of life.

For each of us, there has been such a point when we first began to ask the questions we are still seeking to answer.

11. Looking for Answers

For me, childish questioning about life's mysteries would have to wait for answers.

Only much later in life did I seek to put into words the deep thoughts that circulated in my mind: "What is life all about?" and "Who am I?"

These queries begged an answer.

More than four-fifths into a century of life on planet Earth, I find these questions still only partially answered. I know now that the full answer will come only beyond the grave when I hope to be introduced into the fullness of life in eternity. So long as I live life on Earth, I will be seeking more profound answers.

12. Subtle Changes in Attitude

I am writing now at a point in life when hopes and dreams have been attained, have failed, or have been forgotten.

I am at an age when my body tells me that it is no longer young, that I am old. I tire easily and enjoy a nap after lunchtime.

Yet I am content.

Yes, the media remind me of much injustice, many wrongs, many scandals, but I view all of these concerns in a much different light than I once did.

It is not that I do not care, that I am callous, that I have given up on life. Life is not rosy; it is often painful. But this realization does not disturb me. Rather, I am seeing life from a different perspective now that I am older.

Without my being aware of the shifting of my emphases over the years, time had done that for me.

13. Carefree Earlier Years

In my earlier years, I saw the events of life almost entirely in the light of their relevance to me, their impact on me, not considering how I might alter my circumstances.

I had yet to learn the power within me to direct my life. I had to learn that life has many layers, that there are depths within to be explored.

As mid-life approached and pressures of living in a competitive world became more intense, I realized that life has a deeper meaning than I had yet discerned. Otherwise it would not be worth the pain and the hardships it demanded.

Childhood's wide-eyed questioning had now converted to a sense of urgency about understanding life's meaning.

14. Life's Impact on the Individual

I began to observe other people, noting how they handled the puzzles and contrarieties of life. I saw some become stronger as they met the daily grind and occasional crises. Others I saw who were being destroyed by life's challenges.

I asked myself why adversity made some people better, while it led others to crumble and deteriorate. I wondered what made the difference.

Life tests each of us for courage and endurance. How is it that one person ends up with a permanent frown and another with a heart-warming smile?

Clearly, I could learn something valuable by observing various people's ways of responding to challenges.

15. Challenge to Love

Obviously, life is a challenge, but a challenge to what? With prayer and much probing, I arrived at the conviction that the challenge of life is simply to learn to love.

Bolstered with this insight, I found my attitude toward life taking on new purpose and meaning.

At the same time, what seemed to be such a simple and clear idea at the outset became confusing as I wrestled with it.

What is love? What is the source of love? Do I possess love within myself, or is it communicated to me from outside self?

Why should I love? Under what circumstances should I show love? How do I express love toward myself and toward others?

Seeking answers, I found only more questions.

16. Reaching Out to Others

Searching in Scripture for the way to love could seem to place too idealistic, too lofty a demand on us.

And yet what the life of Jesus models for us is something we have always instinctively known was the right way to act. Without being Scripture scholars, we understood that a good life involves reaching out to others.

Through his incarnation, redemptive death, resurrection, and ascension, Jesus shared with us the ability to love with his own love, with God-love. In Jesus, human actions are divinized. Not only did Jesus give us the command to love one another with his kind of love, but also he shows us how. His words and his actions empower us to meet the challenge he offers. He has so identified himself with us that he considers what is done to even the least of his people as done to himself.

We can encourage ourselves by recalling some tiny thing done for another this very day. Jesus has promised to consider as done to him whatever kindness we extend to another. Not even one cup of water given in his name will go unnoticed or unrewarded.

Believing in this promise, we can be assured of support throughout life in our efforts to meet the challenge to love others as Jesus has loved us.

17. Wise Enough to Love

Age has not just added years and aches and pains. Age has outfitted us with greater wisdom and maturity than we have been able to claim earlier. Seeing life with more mature eyes, we can sift out the important from the unimportant.

Better than we could have understood earlier, we see the challenge to love as both a responsibility to bear and a privilege to strive for, alongside Jesus who is truly the Way.

When we attempt to meet this challenge in our personal living, we rightly do what our greater age demands of us: We respond to the call to greater maturity.

The gift of added years is our invitation from God to continue moving out of our tiny world of youthful self-centeredness and into the wider world of loving relationships with others.

18. Ongoing Search

It is now many years since I looked into my reflected eyes seeking to know what lay behind them, but not knowing how to get my unspoken questions answered. I must still seek the answers to those same basic questions about who I am and what my life is meant to be.

What is it in me that keeps me searching for the good, the true? Day by day, week by week, year by year, my life is unfolding and the joy of discovery continues. I am on the way, following clues, accepting and dispensing love. I am on a lifetime treasure hunt, searching for clues to guide me to that treasure beyond all price.

A child limited in experience but rich in expectancy takes it for granted that every question has an easy and direct answer. The adult has learned not to expect direct answers, but rather to engage in a search for bits and pieces of answers.

God, one might say, is playing hide-and-seek with the adult, challenging and calling forth the best the person is capable of. Willingly entering into such a game already makes one a winner. As I think how often I have missed the clues in this game, I thank God for being patient with me. Perhaps Job can speak for me here:

"I have dealt with things that I do not understand: things too wonderful for me, which I cannot know. I had heard of you by word of mouth, but now my eye has seen you. Therefore I disown what I have said, and repent in dust and ashes" (Job 42:3–6).

The best form my repentance can take is an increasingly loving life, a life that shows I know what love of others means.

19. Questioning

Questioning is the voice of a child testing reality
a student seeking the answer
an adolescent searching for his own identity
a sculptor chiseling toward a perfect work
the poet speaking of beauty
the scientist probing nature's secrets
the philosopher ever looking for truth
Job encountering suffering.

Questioning is a way to the unknown
a font of knowledge
a source of wisdom
growth through learning, testing, proving.

Questioning is humanity's constant companion:
thirst that can never be slaked
hunger that can never be satisfied
vacuum that can never be filled.

Questioning is humanity's magic words: Why?
Which? What? When? Where? How?

Lacking these words, our lives would be less than
human.

PART THREE

I Have Walked With Them

Individuals are unique—a fact that accounts for much of the delight we find in our acquaintances. And yet we share the human condition and, therefore, have much in common with each other. Others' experiences sometimes can aid our own coping with certain facets of the retirement phenomenon.

20. I Have Walked With Them

Fourteen years before my own retirement, my work immersed me in the lives of people who had reached retirement age. As a minister to the elderly in a Seattle parish, I was in close contact with aging persons of varying degrees of alertness and mobility. People with whom I dealt ranged from those still very active in professions to those in nursing homes.

These experiences both confronted me with the realities of the aging process and also deepened my respect for the aging person.

I saw for myself that an accumulation of years may well bring an assortment of difficulties, but I saw also how admirably many individuals cope with the unaccustomed situations age brings. From such people as these I have gleaned much about ways to age gracefully and even joyfully. To them I owe a debt of gratitude.

21. Aging as a Process

No one period of life, of course, has a monopoly on either joys or sorrows. Life is not compartmentalized. It is a process in which one period merges into the next, building upon what has been. However, aging entails specific limitations that may create a heavy burden for the individual.

The media sometimes characterize the elderly as if all are poor, needy, and neglected, or as if most are wealthy, pampered, and comfortable. Neither picture is realistic, for the aging process touches each individual, whatever his or her economic or social status.

Of course, it is true that material security can alleviate some of the problems age brings. Even the wealthy, however, are not exempt from some of age's commonly experienced problems. Worn-out hearts, stiff muscles, dulled hearing, dimmed sight, lowered energy—these frequent companions of aging can arrive in a palace as easily as in a one-room apartment.

Rich or poor, we feel the effects of our accumulated years. Rich or poor, we yet can choose what shall be the quality of our days during this stage of our lives.

22. I Am More Than What Appears

Physical limitations can isolate the elderly from others around them, even from those with whom they live. Impaired hearing makes conversation difficult and often confusing. Poor sight restricts reading and possibly even television viewing. Weakness and reduced mobility may contract the world of the elderly even further, eliminating the opportunity for the travel and hobbies they had perhaps put off until retirement.

Such inescapable restrictions may alter the focus of a person's life radically, making a mockery of the term "golden years."

Even after a highly successful career, the elderly person may be overlooked or slighted by thoughtless people. Particularly is such treatment likely in a society that idolizes youthfulness and tries to forestall signs of aging. Even the mandatory age levels for retirement may seem an affront to an individual who knows that his aging has not meant deterioration in capability.

The wise person knows that the "I" in the individual has not been erased by the presence of a limp or by the cessation of a public role.

Perhaps it is only with age that some of us learn that one's true identity has very little to do with personal appearance or with position. It may happen that at seventy or eighty we are face to face with our real selves for the first time.

23. Gnawing Intruder: Anxiety

Loneliness and diminished vigor are not the only new realities that age brings. Another quality I have discovered common among the elderly, from whatever walk of life, is anxiety.

Frail health can make even small difficulties threatening, presaging the possibility of total helplessness that would make the person a burden to others. Some worry about being afflicted with the debilitating Alzheimer's disease, especially if the family history suggests the possibility. Many anguish over diminishing memory or faltering steps that may make the "safer" environment of a nursing home their family's decision for them.

Political unrest in the world also causes the elderly anxiety, for their experience has shown them how interdependent are the lives inhabiting planet Earth. They fear financial instability here or abroad that may threaten resources saved over the years and intended for retirement.

They worry about the future of their loved ones in a world that is experiencing dizzying, rapid change. They are well aware of the crimes spawned by joblessness and substance abuse. For themselves, they fear robbery, mugging, physical abuse. Few elderly escape the anguish of fear and anxiety.

Whether through faith in God's providence, through natural disposition, or through stoic survival skills, the fortunate are spared this pain. The past *is* prologue; changing one's thinking patterns now may offset that potential pain.

24. Heroic Courage

The latter years of life offer time to evaluate how well we have learned to appreciate, and to harmonize with, those around us. These years also test our courage.

As I have heard life stories of some of the elderly, I have been filled with admiration—almost awe. These survivors have not been crushed by seemingly insurmountable obstacles, but have succeeded in living rather normal lives—abnormal only for the near-heroic quality they have brought to life's vicissitudes.

Their stories have given concrete reality to abstract terms like *trust, courage, generosity, hope, faith, love,* and *forgiveness.* These are the unsung heroes living among us, testifying to the remarkable resilience and nobility of the human spirit.

These are the exemplars who offer us an ideal as we approach the leisure time of retirement years. If these tried and tested individuals could find life worth living despite having suffered bankruptcy, hunger, the sense-less murder of a teenage son, or betrayal by a trusted friend, certainly all of us can make something positive of extra years granted us—despite the nagging annoyances that come with aging.

25. Our Spirits Found One Another

I have walked with them,
yet never worn their shoes.
I have listened as they spoke
and I have heard,
yet theirs were the woes.

I have sat with them,
but theirs the broken heart.
I have prayed with them,
and in our prayers
our spirits found one another.

PART FOUR

Who Am I Now
That I Am Old and Retired?

Pop psychology has had several generations of clients searching for their identities as a solution to almost any problem. Comics and cartoonists have had a heyday with the concept of self-definition. The retired person may find the matter of identity a serious question, particularly if he or she has long equated "what I do" with "who I am."

26. Who Am I Now?

Now that I am old and retired, I am beginning to wonder who I am.

Not so long ago, this feeling of uncertainty had never entered my mind. I knew who I was. I was the executive secretary. . . or the chief operating officer . . . or a trial lawyer . . . or the head accountant . . . or the director of social services . . . or. . . .

Throughout my career years, my fellow workers and other associates knew me and knew what to expect from me. I had a certain status that identified me.

Now, however, things have changed. I have retired, and someone else has my job, my title, my office. Someone else is doing the work I used to do. Someone else is being sought out for the advice that I used to give. I am sitting on the sidelines watching life go by rather than running an operation. I am no longer needed at the office, at meetings, at conferences.

When morning comes, I can ignore the alarm clock. I don't have to be at any particular place at any particular time. I don't even have to dress up. I don't have to rush to be ready for the carpool pick-up or the subway. I don't have to check to make sure I have my briefcase in hand.

I have retired. I am without a defined job to do today. Who am I now?

27. Blessing in Disguise

Who or what am I supposed to be as a retired person? Could my dilemma result from having too closely associated who I am with what I did? Could it be that I tended to put what I was doing before who was doing the work? Was I immersing myself in the work without thinking of the worker?

Could it be that the real person I am has been hiding behind a professional screen? Have I been wearing a mask without lifting it long enough to find out who is behind it?

If so, this new feeling of uncertainty and confusion may be a blessing, rather than a devastating event in my life. Perhaps the task of my retired years, I tell myself, is to dissociate the person from the work to which I had long committed myself. Properly handled, retirement could be a giant step toward inner freedom.

An analogy can perhaps illustrate this liberating aspect of self-discovery during one's later years. We have all seen a piece of furniture made of excellent wood that had been painted over for some reason. To restore the natural beauty of the wood, one must remove the paint layers. As the paint disappears, the beauty of the grain in the wood begins to reappear. The wood's beauty was there all of the time, but had been hidden by the paint. Freed from the facade, the natural wood could be seen for what it was.

28. The Shaping of This Unique Person

Experiences unique to each of us have contributed to the persons we are today.

Having lived many years, I have necessarily experienced much along the way. All that I have experienced—the people I have known, the activities I have been engaged in, the circumstances of my living situations—has left its mark upon me.

While I am in one sense the same person who began life many decades ago, in another sense I am not the same, for I have been shaped by my life's experiences.

Life may have been "good" to me or may have treated me "badly." I may be sickly or healthy, active or an invalid, with family and friends or without them. I may have financial security or a rather frugal existence. I may be a happy and content person or a frustrated and anxious type of individual.

These facts about me are accidentals that do not change my identity, my person. Still, they figure as contributors to my present personality—that amalgam of traits that reflects how I have dealt with what life has dealt to me.

That indeed is the key to the person I am now. I am, possibly even physically, the one-of-a-kind person I am as a result of the ways I have handled the experiences that make up my unique life.

29. Message from the Sturdy Apple Tree

I like to compare the life span of an elderly person to the growth rings on a long-standing tree.

At some point, a seed found root in the dark soil. Under the influence of sun, rain, and nourishment, the seed sprouted, grew into a sapling, and matured into grand sturdiness and beauty. Weathering storms and seasons, the tree grew strong branches that bore beautiful leaves, blossoms, and fruit. Its shade provided shelter for the traveler, its fruits nourished the hungry, and its limbs provided a play place for children.

Year after year, the seasons turned the leaves from green to yellow, bronze, or red, and then sent them floating to the ground to cover new life hidden there during the cold winter. As the fallen leaves disintegrated, they nourished the soil, which in turn promoted growth of new plant life.

Stripped of its leaves, the tree's strong silhouette against the wintry sky spoke of courage and endurance.

At times, snow ermined its branches, and icicles hung from its twigs like sparkling earrings. Then the snow left behind a skeleton awaiting spring to awaken it.

What had seemed stark and barren during the late winter months sprouted tiny green leaves with spring's arrival. Soon the stalwart tree would be richly decked for another summer of providing shelter, food, and fun.

Only the elderly can appreciate the message of a sturdy tree that remains itself through every season and every condition of its life.

30. Who Are the Elderly?

We are the seedbed of today's flowering.
We are the shadow cast by the sun
   once it has reached its zenith.
We are the mirror of what has been;
We are the voice of our culture's past.
We are the echo of a song that has been sung;
We are the spirit, the heart, the soul,
   the brain, the brawn of today's culture.

We are the have-beens; yet we live on
   in the present we have built.

We are tradition:
   Today's people are born of us,
   Today's stories have come from us,
   Today's ideals have been lived by us,
   Today's future has been created by us.

Our bodies are bent in carrying the load;
Our heads are gray with searching the way;
Our voices are weak from having spoken our line;
Our hands are gnarled from carrying the load;
Our feet are weary from life's long journey;
Our eyes are dim from discerning the future;
Our ears are dull from listening to humanity's cry;
Our lined faces speak who we are.

We are the bridge over which humanity must walk
   on its journey to tomorrow.

PART FIVE

Time to Take Stock

With time on her hands, the retired person may discover many surprising facts about herself and her lifestyle. A professional homemaker may be amazed at the amount of long-forgotten fabric occupying shelf space. The ex-golfer may gasp at the fortune he has spent for golf regalia and equipment that now sit in the basement. Personal habits may become conscious actions for the first time—and some definitely need improvement. Retirement is a time for taking stock.

31. Taking Inventory

Some of us are collectors by nature. We see "value" in everything. Retirement offers the opportunity for new vistas. It is the time to assess our belongings to determine which of them are burdens and which have value for this new phase of life.

Nearly everyone carries around extra baggage—material objects, psychological attitudes, or intellectual habits. The retirement point in life is an ideal time to evaluate one's "holdings."

What can make these years worthwhile? How can retirement time be growth time?

Weeks, months, or even years of addressing these questions may prod one to start winnowing one's lifetime collection, material and intangible.

In some cases, discarding is the best decision. In others, perhaps we should "pare and share." In still other cases, possibly we should increase, reinforce, or alter our holdings.

"Clutter," whether material or psychological, can paralyze a person into deadening passivity and routine. Taking charge of the quality of one's retirement time, on the other hand, keeps life both interesting and rewarding.

32. Too Much Is Too Much

The very act of sorting out what is worth keeping, and what is not, can revitalize retirement time, forcing some important decision making: What shall occupy this new and different time of life with its precious work-free days? No longer can we plead "too busy" for putting off this or that good intention.

During our active work years, we likely spent much time and talent acquiring what we considered necessary for human living: not just food, clothing, and shelter, but also the furnishings and equipment and bric-a-brac that added convenience and perhaps "style" to our environment.

From our parents' example of providing for themselves and us, we had learned to acquire, preserve, protect, augment, and manage a broad range of possessions. In our turn, we have likely far surpassed our parents in the variety and the mass of our holdings.

Not only will our own lives be less cluttered if we sort through our accumulations. The process will likely take us on many a trip down memory lane—making us glad again for the good times . . . and relieved that the tough ones are behind us.

We will also do a favor in advance for our descendants if we—not they—make the decisions about what to do with what we have left behind. That consideration should goad us to action!

33. Another Kind of Assessment

During all of our earlier years, a particular personality was developing, a particular character with a particular set of habits of mind and behavior.

We may feel that inescapable circumstances of birth and opportunity had much to do with shaping that self.

Older now, we face a new period of life when we can dictate its shape and quality to a great extent by the attitudes we bring to it and by the environment we create for ourselves.

Never before in our lives has there been a period when we have been less bounded by the strictures of time and obligation; we are beholden now neither to boss nor to employees. Children no longer claim or need our attention and time.

The time is ours to manage.

While to some extent we may feel constricted by certain ravages of aging itself, can we with honesty plead "age" as an exemption from continued personal growth?

To do so would minimize the value of all that has gone before in our lives. The maturing process of those years was prelude to this very moment.

There is time now to think deeply about becoming the kind of person one really would like to be.

Could there be a better use of available time?

34. Our Gift to Human Ecology

How does one go about using precious time well? Without some kind of conscious decisions on our part, the gift of retirement years can slip by unused and unappreciated. We have not traveled this part of the road before; what steps should we take?

To have a role in designing this uncharted future, we will have to re-set goals to match the new tasks ahead.

Put very simply, this is a time for deciding what shall fill our minds, our hearts, our days, and even our living space day after day for the years ahead.

With fewer and less pressing duties to distract us, we can let the insights gained from a wealth of experience direct our judgment about making these the best years of our lives.

In one sense, we might see the retirement years as "tidying up time" after the foundation years of earning a livelihood. Just as a builder takes down the scaffolding once the structural lines of the new edifice are well in place, so should the elderly person stand back and consider whether the time has arrived to rid herself of props no longer meaningful.

Is it not time to add the finishing touches that will make the human edifice the best that it can be? One well might consider each effort a contribution to human ecology.

Our corner of the world will be the better for our having been in it.

35. Taking Stock

When I appraise the trinkets
to which I yet cling,
I am astounded.

These baubles once had value,
were once essential:
I am astounded.

Their meaning escapes me,
their value is zero.
I am astounded.

As cheese on a pizza refuses to let loose,
I have held fast to worthless little nothings.
I am astounded.

I have clung to each object
for weal or for woe.
I cling yet . . . and am astounded.

PART SIX

The Art of Letting Go

Anyone who thinks retirement is the end of work days
has a surprise in store. Possibly the most valuable work
of a lifetime may occur now that a person comes face to
face with the personality and character shaped by the
previous years. The public career may be over, but there
may be tasks ahead that are far more interesting and far
more rewarding. This will definitely be "an inside job."

36. Let the Butterfly Emerge

Viewed as a challenge, retirement is not the end of one's professional life. It is just a change of jobs. The work years are far from over; the work ahead is just of a different kind.

There is much to be done.

The time has come to empty oneself of bitterness, of envy, of selfishness, of a drivenness that may have let one overlook the feelings of others.

It is time for the gentler side of oneself to flower. Perhaps there is yet time to mend some fences, to right some wrongs, to re-establish some valued human connections.

Of course, it is quite possible at this juncture in life to make a quite different choice: to withdraw from others, to retreat comfortably within oneself, and to let the rest of the world go by.

Worse yet, one could become bitter and self-pitying, wasting precious time in bemoaning the lost past.

Either of these options would result in a self-defeating kind of existence. If, for self-protection, we have woven a cocoon about ourselves, it is now time to let the butterfly emerge. It is in freeing the self, in emptying the self, that we can be open to receive the life-expanding gifts of friendship, peace, happiness, new ideas, a deeper kind of living. Shrouded in a cocoon, we would not grow.

37. Stay in the Driver's Seat

It may be helpful to recall that the retirement stage of life really began in our late mid-life, so we have come to it not wholly unprepared.

The process has been much like the operation of a car on a down-grade. As it descends, we brake slightly. However, at the bottom of the hill as we maneuver the car into our driveway, we brake completely and turn off the ignition. We are home.

Reaching retirement age is a feat in itself, and we should have a satisfying feeling of accomplishment at this point—but also a sense of a challenge to handle the time ahead skillfully. After all, parking a car has not disabled it; the vehicle is still there ready to run again, but possibly in new directions.

Perhaps a new retiree selects the wisest course when she consciously determines to decide what shall constitute the focus of this piece of life. Part of that focus, as suggested earlier, ought to be letting go of what is no longer needed or useful.

However, "letting go" is not the same as not caring. In no way should retirement mean just coasting along, relinquishing to others the control of the direction of one's life.

Letting go does not mean giving up. Rather, letting go is "letting God," that is, accepting God's (and nature's) place in our lives. We accept age as a fact, but we also accept that we are still responsible for the direction we take as we travel along.

We are still in the driver's seat.

38. Accentuate the Positive

At sixty or at ninety years old, we are exactly what our responses to all of our decades of living have made us.

Each of us has an inner world which is the amalgam of our life's unique patterning of joys and sorrows and our responses to them. In this inner world is imprinted indelibly, in a personally coded system, what we have experienced since the beginning of life.

Some of those experiences we can recall; others have become submerged in our unconscious, but are no less influential. All that we have absorbed during our lives, consciously or unconsciously, is exerting an influence on us today.

To this network of influences can be attributed our mannerisms, carriage, facial expressions, attitudes, choice of conversation topics, vocabulary, interpretation of events, the quality of our relationships, our ambitions, our use of time, and our attitudes toward ourselves, toward society and individuals, and toward God.

Real and powerful as these forces have been, just as real is our ability to choose the course of our lives and of our growth. What is good and positive can be retained, and what is negative and detrimental can be rejected.

The choice is up to us.

39. Eliminate the Negative

As we prayerfully accept ourselves as we are, we may become aware of negative attitudes at work in us. We may begin to realize that some actions of others that we had registered as purposely injurious to us were really projections of our own negativism that we have attached to their motives.

This kind of insight is a great blessing that stirs us to let go of attitudes that hinder us from growing. We might ask ourselves what accounts for our negative attitudes.

Even under the best of circumstances, nearly every human being carries bruises to the psyche long after the damaging incident has been forgotten. The pain may result from a childhood experience that has never been resolved and that, therefore, is still buried in the subconscious.

We may at some time have considered ourselves unjustly treated by parents, teachers, peers; we may have been the butt of jokes; we may have been (or felt) discriminated against; we may have suffered abuse.

In addition, our career years may have had their own kinds of trauma: excessive demands, heavy competition, boredom on the job.

Whatever the cause, we carry within us the perceived hurt, antipathy, dislike, mistrust, hatred, fear—any of which responses may have warped our personality and likely have diminished our enjoyment of life.

Whatever the problem, whatever the source of the problem, so long as life is within us there is time to let go of the negative burden and get on with living.

40. Feeling Right With God

Perhaps one of the heavier burdens that can sadden a person in the later years is the discovery (or perhaps, at last, the admission) that a gap exists between the self presented to others and the real self inside—known only to God.

We may have considered ourselves fortunate that others could not see the inner domain, but we now feel an urgency to "square up" with God.

Whether or not we have ever adverted to this fact, our relationship with the God who gave us life is the central fact of our existence. What others may think of us is incidental; what God knows of us predicts our eternity.

Letting go of any obstacle that hinders that most basic of relationships can only improve the quality of life.

God has always known our true selves and will unfailingly recognize the prodigal daughter or son, no matter how late the return.

Feeling "right with God" is a blessing par excellence at any stage of life, but certainly it must be a prime value for a person definitely nearing the glorious moment of meeting God face to face. A peaceful heart can look forward to a joyous "Welcome home!"

In a sense, though, for the person freed from material and spiritual clutter, heaven has already begun.

41. Harmony With All
of God's Creation

I awoke last night and felt Earth
breathing in her sleep.

From within her womb came tremors
of molten rock tossing in constraint,
Her structural plates edging and re-positioning,
re-creating Earth's design.
I heard water coursing, finding its way
among rocks and caverns.
I saw tiny creatures burrowing a home,
creating tiny tremors all their own.
I heard the night winds whisper of feathered fowl,
of beasts of prey, of field and flower.
I saw the stars move in their silent course,
and I heard galaxies beyond sight
inviting Earth to share in their dance
with rhythmed harmony.
Surely I could feel at home in this Creation
dancing its cosmic step through time and space,
Shaping for me beauty beyond measure,
gifting me with hints of my Maker's love.
God-Creator, I thank you for my glorious task
of loving you in reverent awe.

PART SEVEN

Travelers on the Way Home

Conscious of the passage of time, we comment, "Time just seems to fly." Aware of the seeming speed with which the days and hours disappear, are we equally aware where the vanishing time is leading us?

42. On the Way Home

Each of us is a traveler on the way home. To find guidance for the journey through time and into eternity, we can do no better than to look into the pages of the Bible.

In the Old Testament, we find the record of our ancestors as they moved through their pilgrimage, both as a people and also as individuals.

Scripture's pages offer tales of courage and of weakness, of faith and of failings, of sin and of virtue. There we find the record of the bond that grew between some of our ancestors and their God, and there we find lessons intended also for us as we continue on our own pilgrimage.

We discern in the Bible the pattern of our ancestors' response to Yahweh's dealings with them. Scripture traces the gradual progress our ancestors made in their understanding of Yahweh, the God who continually opened their eyes to their preciousness in the sight of their creator.

We see them growing in awareness of their dependence on God for their very existence. In their God they found all-embracing and never-failing love.

Our biblical ancestors viewed the time on Earth as a testing ground for a greater life to come. They viewed the human life-span as covenant time with the God on whose fidelity they could depend.

The covenant is still guaranteed. God is always faithful.

43. Call to Fidelity

Through the ages, God has sent prophets to call the people back to fidelity when they had fallen into idolatrous practices.

We read of God's making a covenant with Abraham and then renewing that loving bond through Moses and other chosen leaders. Closer to our times, the covenant was sealed by the mission of God's own Son to share our humanity and thus show us how to live.

Our ancestors were women and men of flesh and blood who voiced their feelings and poured out their desires, fears, and triumphs. A nomadic people, they sought a place of rest during their many journeyings. They longed for a home, a place of stability and peace.

How easily we can identify with these wanderers, for we, too, seek stability amid the changing conditions of our lives. Our search operates on all levels of our being: physical, emotional, intellectual, and spiritual. The search engages us at every stage of our development.

As elderly people, we are yet on our way; we are yet searching.

Well might we review the experience of the biblical wanderers to freshen our sense of our covenant with God.

44. The One Thing Necessary

The psalmist quotes Ecclesiastes (12:8) about the pointlessness of a life lived without thought of God: "Vanity of vanities . . . all things are vanity." Summing up the message, the writer urges a reverent recognition of the one thing necessary: "Fear God, and keep God's commandments; for this is our all" (12:13).

Psalm 71 (1–3,5) records the prayer of an elderly person who has not found life easy, but whose spirit is aglow with trust in God.

In you, O Lord, I take refuge;

let me never be put to shame.

In your justice rescue me, and deliver me;

incline your ear to me and save me.

Be my rock of refuge, a stronghold to give me safety,

for you are my rock and my fortress. . . .

For you are my hope, O Lord.

Recalling that he has trusted in God "from birth," the petitioner (Psalm 71:9–11) asks to be assisted also through his later years:

Cast me not off in my old age;

as my strength fails, forsake me not,

for my enemies speak against me,

and they who keep watch against my life take counsel.

They say, "God has forsaken him;

pursue and seize him,

for there is no one to rescue him."

But the psalmist knows better. There is always Someone to come to the rescue. That assurance is the blessing that faith in God brings.

45. New Testament Light

As do so many words of Scripture, Psalm 42 and Psalm 43 let us feel with those who have lived a faith-life before us. The writers—our ancestors in faith—brought to God their trials, their fears, their yearnings, their heartaches, but they survived because they also approached God with hope and trust.

The New Testament resonates perhaps even more closely with our deepest longings because the person of Jesus makes God's love for us inescapably believable.

Delving more and more deeply into that ever-remarkable record of God-with-us in the person of Jesus, such as the disciples walking with Jesus toward Emmaus (Luke 24:32), we find our own hearts burning within us with excitement and hope and joy; for, indeed, in Jesus we have a guide, a model, a savior.

If we need a renewal of appreciation for the almost too-good-to-be-true fact that God's own son has lived on Earth, we need only reacquaint ourselves with the pages left by those sharers of the Good News: Matthew, Mark, Luke, and John.

Rereading their records of Jesus' thirty-three years on Earth, we can warm our hearts once again with gratitude to a God who has loved us so much as to send the Divine Son to be our model and guide.

Refreshing ourselves with the familiar record is sure to rekindle our first excitement about being the beloved of God.

46. God With Us and We With God

It is amazing: We live in that time between Jesus' coming to Earth two thousand years ago and his promised return in the future. At Bethlehem he came in humility and embraced a life of suffering. On his return, he will come in glory to judge those he laid down his life for.

Our time on Earth is travel time; we are travelers on the way home. Some of us are nearer the journey's end than others, but we can envision it as only the beginning of another, and even better, life in eternity. And we have Jesus as companion, for he is Emmanuel: God with us.

What will this new life be like? Will we find what we have longed for? Will we find that perfect "home" we seek? Will we reach that stillpoint in our being in which peace reigns?

Jesus himself, in his last discourse, has assured us that we will find all of this. At the Last Supper, Jesus had just told his apostles that he was going away. Peter asked, "Where do you mean to go?" Jesus replied, "I am going where you cannot go now; later on you shall come after me" (John 13:36). Then he added these heart-lifting words for his followers then and now (John 14:1–3):

"Do not let your hearts be troubled. Have faith in God and faith in me. In my Father's house there are many dwelling places; otherwise, how could I have told you that I was going to prepare a place for you? I am indeed going to prepare a place for you, and then I shall come back to take you with me, that where I am you also may be."

The travelers will have reached their true homeland.

47. On the Way Home

(Today's joggers and commuters are intent on their goals, although with a less poetic approach than the psalmist attributed to people of his day. I might ask myself if I run with as much earnestness as either group.)

Daily I watch them, these joggers,
Pass my window at 5:30 A.M. sharp—
Elbows at side, heads held high.
They jog.

They are going somewhere and they know the way,
Around the corner and down the road.
After a mile or so
I'll see them again.

Daily I watch them, these commuters,
Pass my window on the freeway below.
Bumper to bumper at 5:30 P.M.
They move.

They are going somewhere and they know the way,
Around the corner and down the freeway.
At 5:30 P.M. sharp tomorrow
I'll see them again.

Daily I watch them, family and friends,
Within my mind's eye; I call each by name.
Faces uplifted, eyes set on the goal,
They travel.

They are going somewhere and they know the way.
Carrying their burden, avoiding pitfalls,
They travel light:
They are on the way home.

PART EIGHT

Those Who Mourn: The Widowed

The very word "widowed" is packed with memories. Individuals burdened with that experience need no one to tell them of the flood of feelings this status calls forth. Those who have not had the experience can learn to be of help to the widowed through a caring empathy.

48. Initial Shock

When death takes away a longtime companion, life for the remaining partner undergoes massive change. Widowed persons have told me that losing a spouse in death is like losing part of oneself.

This is especially true for those whose marriages had grown into close, loving relationships extended over many years. After pledging themselves to each other for life, they shared each day's great and small happenings and their two lives had blended into one.

Now death had intervened, and the other is no longer there to share joys, sorrows, successes, failures, surprises, jokes. No longer could one partner turn to that other trusted person for suggestions, for a listening ear, for a sharing of thoughts and moods.

The initial response of one widowed is shock. Sometimes the bereaved person is dazed, not grasping what has taken place—even if the death had been foreseen.

Sometimes the emotions seem frozen; the individual functions as usual, making appropriate responses and decisions, and is thought to be "handling this pretty well." But the person is on "automatic pilot": acting out of habit to cope with a fact too great to be grasped yet.

During the first days so much has to be done and friends are so attentive that the full impact of the loss has not struck home.

Only on dropping back into what should be normal living does the individual come face to face with the reality: a life in disarray.

Only those who have been there can know the pain.

49. Necessity for Grieving

Whether one is widowed while young, middle-aged, or elderly, the event signals a turning point and a new direction. Life is not the same as it was before.

The shock of separation may at first dull a person's perceptions of the present moment, but eventually the startling new situation brings one face to face with the large realities of life, both those of the moment and those yet to be faced.

This major change calls forth soul-searching, a time that can open memory doors, awaken emotions, and stir up regrets—even when these regrets are totally unwarranted.

Life is out of joint, and the widowed person needs time to grieve.

Cultural customs throughout the ages have recognized this need and have provided a time and a protocol for grieving and healing.

Unfortunately, today's America seems to shy away from incorporating a grieving period into its approach to death. Yet the widowed person needs time, space, friends, and support groups that provide solace and encouragement during the transition time following a death.

Learning to be quiet listeners and companions is the best help one can offer at a time that is intensely personal and individual for the person coming to terms with such grief.

---

50. Facing the Reality

Some helpful customs for assisting bereaved people are available today. Churches and funeral arrangers offer help. Also, institutions and groups increasingly offer programs and support groups for the grieving.

Still, one must question the wisdom of customs that gloss over the reality of death. For example, the seriousness of the reality facing the grieving person is purposely dimmed by the soothing colors and the plush setting of the funeral parlor. Bright floral bouquets, the bereaved person's favorite musical selections, and upbeat personal testimonials all tend to dull the recognition that a death, a painful separation, has occurred.

The family and friends must not see the coffin lowered into the ground or covered with dirt. The increasing choice of cremation and the use of a mausoleum tend to distance and to depersonalize what is an intensely personal loss to the bereaved spouse.

Healing comes only when truth is honored.

Perhaps the widowed who have survived the experience could band together to evaluate how society and friends can best provide what is needed at the time of loss: permission and space for the griever to face reality and grieve, but also support of a kind that will lessen the pain and assist the grieving process.

51. Delayed Grief

Reactions to a partner's death vary, but sooner or later the grieving process must be gone through if healing is to occur. For most, the grieving period follows immediately upon the death and will last for an unpredictable time, sometimes mercifully brief, but often for as long as five years.

For others, the grieving will be deferred. A person accustomed to being always in command—controlled and self-assured—may hide the inner turmoil that has taken over. Fearing to show vulnerability and loneliness, he may let a confident front convince even himself that all is going very well. Such a person may function in this manner for a year or longer, but some occasion or other will break open the flood gates of inner reserve and control. Sometimes this burst of feeling comes as a surprise, for the triggering occasion may seem to have no connection with the person mourned.

One widow who had this experience was on a bus when suddenly and unexpectedly she burst into tears and began to weep loudly and violently. What caused her pent-up feelings at this particular moment?

Afterward, she could not recall just what had triggered the reaction. As the bus moved along, something she had seen or remembered or smelled caught her off guard, and the long repressed feelings would no longer remain under her control.

It is wise to recognize that repressed grief will find its way to the surface. Over-activity or stoic endurance only delays the grieving process; it does not supplant it.

52. Make No Major Changes

Feeling restless and sad, some widows and widowers want to make major changes in their lives, anything to avoid the pain of continuing in the old circumstances without the comfort of their companion. They may want to sell the house, move to another location, possibly make changes in handling their finances.

Advice from those with experience is this: "Wait one year before making any major changes." By this time, life will probably have taken on more stability and the individual will be better able to make sound decisions.

But one change must be made without much delay: Clear the house of the belongings of the deceased person, except for a favorite memento. Rearrange the furniture and make the house fit both present needs and personal tastes.

How can one help a grieving friend? Being an interested listener is the best gift. By sympathy one can enter into the feelings of the other and allow him or her to pour forth a spectrum of feelings: bitterness, anger, resentment, self-pity, distrust, guilt, remorse, confusion.

The best and most useful gift for the mourner is to listen without rebuttal and without reproving the other for having those feelings. By entering into the other's feelings, a friend can move a step closer and identify with that person. A friend can help fill those empty moments when the suffering person might otherwise engage in activity for activity's sake . . . or in deep depression.

Such a precious gift to a grieving friend costs only caring and time.

53. Decision Making

A grieving friend may need to be reassured that what is going on within him or her is not imaginary, but quite real and quite understandable in view of the recent loss. The friend can verify that these thoughts and feelings are not a matter for shame just because they are contrary to the person's usual disposition.

The friend's sympathy should not be "soft," but supportive. The aim must be to help the griever gradually regain control of life. It may be necessary to assist the person in arriving at decisions. The friend can suggest alternatives and offer pros and cons of one suggestion or another, but must leave the decisions to the griever.

Laying down a program for the other to follow is not conducive to the healing needed; the afflicted person must be assisted to take on the responsibility of making decisions, whatever his or her role was before the spouse's death.

The surviving spouse may even ask that the friend make decisions, outline a route to follow, take on some of the tasks the bereaved person finds difficult. Within reason, a friend might offer to assist with this, but only as a sidekick—not as the principal. He or she would help by being there and encouraging the griever, but not by taking over the decision-making role.

54. Useful Reading

Sometimes a friend can provide help for someone in mourning. It might be a small item—a pamphlet or a small card with a scriptural message—that brings the grieving person comforting thoughts during lonely hours, and keeps the mourner on the path that is most likely to offer healing.

I came upon a small leaflet that I have offered to mourners: "I Will Trust You, God," by Paul F. Keller and published by Kairos, Box 24306, Minneapolis, Minnesota 55424. Most recipients found it helpful. It contains sixty short meditations to help the person through the first two months after a loss.

The author reminds the reader to trust the spiritual dimension of recovery: "One thing certain about recovery and healing is that without the spiritual emphasis the healing is incomplete, leaving deep wounds which fester for the remainder of our lives here on Earth."

The straightforward purpose of such daily reflections is to lead the person to trust God, to know that God wants the mourner to recover. A reminder of this kind can sometimes help to give direction to a life that has somewhat lost its focus. A creative friend could help make a difference with such an offer.

55. Releasing the Spouse

Much of the work in the mourning process involves releasing the spouse taken by death.

The funeral and the burial have demonstrated the finality of death, yet time is needed for the survivor to let the spouse go. The mind may have learned to accept the fact of the death, but the whole emotional life still awaits adjustment to the new reality. Praying for the deceased partner maintains a link with the person but does not make up for the loss of physical presence.

The "letting go" process does not happen once and for all; each day brings situations that call once again for the act of letting go. For example, when an important decision must be made, the grief returns because the partner is not there to discuss the feasibility of one choice or another.

Or a friend calls to offer an invitation to dinner. Suddenly the thought of going alone to join an intact couple is too much to bear—and the anguish is back. Once again, one must try to let go and get on with life— without a partner.

Life has indeed been altered and will never be the same again.

However, a real life is again possible, but not without some painful effort. As with any change, it is necessary to harness one's reserve of coping measures and move forward.

56. Never Really Separated

Out of sight and even out of conscious remembrance at times, the memory of the beloved deceased partner is still part of the fabric of the bereaved and cannot be erased or ignored into oblivion.

Even a second marriage does not change the fact that what has been before will ever be part of that person. Memories of good times and bad have helped to shape that person even after he or she has begun a new life. As time goes by, a sense of humor and gratitude can convert the past into a source of pleasure rather than pain.

For those with faith in Jesus Christ, it is helpful to recall his compassion for those who suffer. On one occasion he stopped a funeral procession to console the widowed mother of a son being carried out for burial. Not only did Jesus console the grieving woman, but he even gave her son back to her alive. The Lord felt sorry for her. "Don't cry," he said. Then he put his hand on the bier and said, "Young man, I tell you to get up." And the young man sat up and began to speak, and Jesus gave him to his mother (Luke 7:13–16).

Surely the God-Man who showed such compassion continues to care about the anguish of any bereaved person and can bring solace to grieving hearts.

At the same time, God does indeed help those who help themselves. When we learn to recall the departed partner with joyful memories rather than with self-pity, we honor that dear person and are not really separated because a happy recollection brightens the day with loving gratitude.

57. The Healer

(Sometimes a soft, furry kitten can bring moments of
contentment to us. Here, a tiny robin is asked to bear
"the burden of my aching heart.")

Thou little bride of nature,
Come close.
Take all my heavy thoughts
And each one hide
Beneath a feather of your crimson breast.
Then, quickened by your blitheness,
Let them ride there
Through sunshine, mist and shade,
My little guide.
Then bring them back warm and weary
At eventide

To ease the burden of my aching heart.

PART NINE

Suffering Can Transform

Suffering touches every human life. What we decide to do with our personal suffering has much to do with the quality of our lives.

58. The Mystery of Suffering

No person who has survived into retirement years needs to be told that suffering is a reality of life. What we often cannot understand is the reason for suffering.

Ancient peoples associated suffering with evil, as something of a penalty for someone's wrongdoing. This was indeed the accepted view in Jesus' time, but he set about to correct that idea. We see his reaction not only in his attitude toward sinners and sufferers in general, but in particular cases. The evangelist John recounts an instance that still today cautions against equating suffering with punishment for wrongdoing.

As he went along, Jesus saw a man who had been blind since birth. His disciples asked him, "Rabbi, was it his sin or that of his parents that caused him to be born blind?" "Neither," answered Jesus: "It was no sin, either of this man or of his parents. Rather, it was to let God's works show forth in him" (John 9:1–3).

Jesus seems to endorse the idea that suffering is an evil, but he corrects the assumption that the sufferer or his parents can be blamed for the occurrence of this evil. As with other aspects of the human condition, suffering demands from us an appropriate response. Suffering may be a mystery, but the necessity to cope with it is a simple fact of life.

59. Patient Job

The Book of Job struggles with the mystery of suffering, particularly in instances when a just person suffers. That person tends to ask, "Why me, Lord?"

Job's conversion of heart suggests the appropriate attitude of the sufferer toward God and pain. Job is a person of good name, much wealth, and sound health; his family is blessed with many sons and daughters. Life is pretty much what one might expect for a faithful servant of Yahweh.

Suddenly and unexpectedly, Job loses all: possessions, family, honor, and health.

Hearing of his misfortune, three of his friends come to comfort him. They sit silently with Job day and night for seven days before he speaks a word. In his anguish, Job at last cries out, "I regret I was ever born." One by one, his friends suggest the remedy they consider obvious: Job should acknowledge the sin that has brought such misfortune upon him.

Job protests his innocence. The three finally give up their effort to help; they cannot convince Job that he is hiding the sin that has brought this punishment upon him.

Then a younger man, Elihu, takes his turn trying to pry the "truth" from Job. As might be expected, the innocent Job receives no comfort from Elihu, since the young man does not understand the mystery of suffering—any more than we do. Job will need enlightenment from a different source.

And so may we.

60. God to Job's Rescue

Finally, Yahweh speaks to Job, "Who are you, obscuring my designs with your empty-headed words? Brace yourself; now it is my turn to ask questions and yours to inform me" (Job 38:2–3). Yahweh asks Job many questions about the mysteries of the universe. Unable to answer, Job humbly acknowledges Yahweh's sovereign domain. Chastened, Job apologizes for his mistrust of his Maker: "I knew you then only by hearsay, but now I have seen you with my own eyes. I retract all I have said, and in dust and ashes I repent" (Job 42:5–6).

Then the happy conclusion: Yahweh restores Job's fortunes, because he has prayed for his friends. More than that, Yahweh gives him double of what he had before. And all of Job's brothers and sisters and friends of former times come to see him and sit down at table with him. They show him every sympathy and comfort him for all the evil Yahweh had inflicted on him (Job 42:10–11).

The Book of Job drives home a basic truth: Unaided human intelligence is incapable of comprehending the mystery of suffering. However, Jesus' redemptive passion, death, and resurrection contain the complete answer to the mystery of suffering in human life. In itself, suffering is meaningless, but united to the redemptive sufferings of Jesus, it is of infinite value. Those who meet the suffering Jesus in their own pain and darkness are able to rise with him in his resurrected life.

Even Job recognized suffering's power to transform. Suffering had let him see God with his own eyes.

61. Logic Not Enough

Reason says that suffering is an evil to be avoided at all costs, but faith goes beyond reason. Faith, which acknowledges Jesus' redemptive gift to humankind, sheds light on the meaning and purpose of suffering. Jesus himself found suffering repugnant; he asked his Father that he might be spared his suffering: "Father, if you are willing, take this cup from me. Nevertheless, let your will be done, not mine" (Luke 22:42–43).

Ever obedient to his Father, Jesus endured the passion for the salvation of us all, making it possible to unite our sufferings with his.

Of themselves, our sufferings have no redemptive value. Yet, when united to his through faith and conscious intention, ours too have redemptive meaning. Accepted in faith, our sufferings become real treasures—although under an unpleasant disguise. St. Paul grasped the transforming power of suffering borne in union with Jesus: "What we suffer in this life can never be compared to the glory, as yet unrevealed, which is waiting for us" (Romans 8:18).

We do not, however, have to wait for eternity to see some of the positive effects of suffering. Pain and hardships can transform the life of the individual who accepts these sufferings as an invitation to an intimate, loving relationship with Jesus, who is ever the Way.

62. Ministry of Compassion

Compassionate individuals strike me as people who have arrived at a second springtime in their lives. There is a special something about compassionate people that defies description, but sets them a cut above the ordinary. They seem at peace with themselves and non-judgmental about others. A certain warm and gentle reverence toward others makes anyone feel at ease and welcome in their presence.

Such compassionate individuals come from all walks of life, from every culture, every profession. Some are actively employed, some retired, some suffering, and some bedridden.

Such compassion is evident in attitudes adopted toward others and toward our shared human condition.

In a newssheet published by a Seattle shelter for the homeless, I found an example of this kind of presence to others. An acquaintance, the writer said, stopped in on a bitterly cold day and joined the homeless who had gathered at the corner coffee bar for warmth and companionship. Their pretensions long dissipated, the poor took her in as one of their own.

I realized that the ministry of presence is practiced by these homeless people. . . . Steam rose from the coffee to warm them all as they discussed their problems.

With no questions asked, the "regulars" had taken in the stranger. Somehow their lives had taught them the lesson Job's life had taught him.

63. The Day of Life

All day long in color, life, and effulgence,
In activity, beauty, movement, and repose,
The sun has elicited from nature a riot of energy.
And nature has, in turn, played upon my senses,
Evoking all the light and energy of my soul's powers.
These, in turn, have praised, blessed, loved, and
Thanked the Creator of such magnificence.

Now, with the sun's declining hours,
Nature's wonders sink, not to rest, but to retire
As courtiers of the magni-ruler of the day.

My soul, bereft of color, light, and gaiety
Sits widowed by my numbed, dulled senses.
A gnawing longing nibbles at my senses
And betrays my lonely vulnerability.
Shall my soul in silence, sense-starved,
Sit and wait and wait—a desolate lover—
Upon the doorstep of the unseen Beloved?

The answer comes: Yes, wait, for he will come:
This Lover who indulgently splashes beauty
On walls and in corners of his child's playhouse.

PART TEN

That Five-Letter Word

Death is like a shadow, a steady companion of life. We gladly embrace and discuss life, but we avoid bringing its companion—death—to the forefront of our consciousness.

64. Dealing With a Taboo

As with those forbidden four-letter words, one five-letter word is never really taught to us explicitly; yet each of us becomes aware of it some time in life. Its reality is with us from the very beginning of life, but only gradually do we become conscious of the word and, later yet, the experience.

Treated almost as a taboo, the word "death" does not easily enter a vocabulary or a conversation. Parents hesitate to bring the term directly into a child's vocabulary, putting it off until the child can "handle" the idea. Still, even small children come to know of the reality, often in the death of a pet. Some children learn of it at a much deeper level when they lose a parent, another member of the family, or a friend.

Like it or not, death is a shadow that accompanies us throughout life. Most of the time it conveniently keeps out of our direct vision. However, let some life-threatening encounter occur and we find ourselves looking directly into its face.

Our inborn sense of self-preservation has made us cautious of anything that might endanger us, so, in a sense, we are ever aware of this threatening shadow. In more thoughtful moments, we may occasionally give a few fleeting moments to the certainty of death. Yet, thankfully, we spend the greater part of our time in the more productive activity of living.

65. Two Opposing Views of Death

Our mortality is a fact; we know this. And yet, during youth and young maturity we scarcely give death a thought. In later years the reality presses upon our consciousness when we see friends our own age die or when we note in ourselves some indications of advancing years. We know for certain that death is ahead for us at some point, but most of us stave off the thought as effectively as we can.

Most of us entertain one or other of two views on death. Those who have throughout their lives thought of earthly life as the preamble to a heavenly life tend to look forward to death, envisioning it as the gateway to heaven. Those who have concentrated their efforts and thoughts on transitory possessions and treasures of this life dread the approach of death, viewing it as a thief that will deprive them of what they now cherish.

Most of us elderly fit somewhere between those two extremes. I think of my own mother shortly before her death, reflecting on that coming event.

She said, "I can hardly wait to get across, but I do not like the crossing."

None of us likes the thought that death is ahead for us. Many people fear death, for it terminates all we now know.

Small wonder that we do not care for a reality which will bring to an end the world as we know it and which tells us of nothing that will be granted in exchange for the loss.

66. Death Doesn't Make Sense

Only the gift of faith can fill the vacuum created by death. Our trust in a benevolent God assures us that there is something greater beyond than what we have here and now.

If we are in awe of creation's vastness, beauty, and power, we try to imagine an even greater reality in the great beyond. If we marvel at the technology that can reveal the secrets of the universe, from the structure of the invisible atom to the expanse of planets and stars, we ponder what can exceed the wonders the human mind has discovered.

These marvels also pose a dilemma. If the human body is a marvel of design and functioning, what benefit is there in letting death still the body's movements, allowing it then to decay?

Why does the creator allow death to separate us from consciousness of the wonders we have spent our lives absorbing? Why has God made Earth so beautiful if we must leave it? Why has God commanded us to love one another if death will bring separation?

Humanly speaking, death just does not make sense. When human logic doesn't work, faith and trust must fill the gap.

67. Mortality Can't Be the Whole Story

What is certain about death is that it happens. What is uncertain is the time, the occasion, the aftermath. No one who has gone into the beyond has returned to give us an account of it.

However, Elisabeth Kübler-Ross and others have told of persons who have reported having had a near-death experience and then returning to consciousness with an account of what they recall.

The fact is, though, that each of these had yet to face the finality of death. If these individuals indeed experienced dying, they had not experienced definitive death, from which there is no return.

Still, something in the human spirit insists that this life-that-ends-in-death cannot be all; some kind of life must follow physical death, or our highest aspirations would be meaningless.

If we believe in God as our creator, we cannot understand God's purpose in giving life and intelligence to us only to extinguish these gifts at death. Not only faith, but our reason also reaffirms our inner voice that insists there must be life beyond this life.

68. Promise of Eternal Life

Death is a harsh reality for those left behind, as the historical Jesus obviously recognized. Jesus compassionately exercised the power of his divinity by countermanding death on several occasions. Jesus raised the daughter of Jairus from the dead: "Little girl, I tell you to get up" (Mark 5:41); he restored to life the son of a widow with his commanding words: "Young man, I tell you to get up" (Luke 7:14).

He made use of another such miraculous intervention on behalf of Mary and Martha when they mourned the loss of their brother Lazarus. Because he cared about the dejection of Lazarus's sisters, Jesus assured them that their weeping was unnecessary: their brother would live.

Pragmatic Martha believed Jesus' promise that her brother would rise again, but she thought he referred only to life beyond death. Jesus consoled her for the present life with his miraculous delivery of Lazarus from the bonds of physical death. His reassuring words also ring down the centuries to bring solace to us as we contemplate our own mortality: "I am the resurrection and the life. If anyone believes in me, even though he dies he will live, and whoever lives and believes in me will never die" (John 11:25–26).

We have today a record of Jesus' uplifting promise of eternal life for those who believe. We have his own word that death leads to new life.

69. Accepting Our Mortality

It may seem presumptuous for anyone to write of death since none of us has firsthand knowledge of it. Yet death is a decisive point in the human experience and it is therefore an important reality we must face. At some point we have to recognize our mortality and consider the implications of this fact.

Faith tells us to trust fully in the God who has given us the Son as a redemption for us all. The incarnated Son loved us to the end of his life, which was plagued by misunderstanding and suffering.

But the risen and ascended Jesus has not left us orphaned; he left us his Spirit to be our guide as we live out our allotted days. And the record of Jesus' experiences on Earth shows us what is true and good and valuable in this life.

So while the shadow of death may continue to be our companion throughout life, its dominion over us has been broken. Because of Jesus, our death is no longer just the termination of earthly life, but also the door to eternal life.

As the apple blossom withers and dies only to be replaced by the luscious fruit, so our life on Earth terminates to allow us to enter into the fruits of our life for all eternity. What glorious wonders a loving God must have awaiting us!

70. A Glimpse Into Our Own Future

Presence at a holy, peaceful death can be a helpful encounter with the spiritual world. Being with my mother at the moment of her death was that for me.

As my mother lay in bed dying, my father knelt on one side of the bed and I on the other. My priest-brother stood at the foot of the bed, holding a crucifix and watching mother carefully.

As her last moments drew near, he raised his hands over her in a final absolution. She had given him his natural life; now he stood near, invoking the eternal merits of the Risen Jesus on her as she entered unending life. Quietly, without apparent struggle of any kind, she slipped away from us.

A peace settled over us. In spite of our inescapable sense of loss, we felt a triumphant joy; we felt more like singing than weeping. Something of the glorious new life she had entered spilled over into us as we shared that blessed moment.

Of course, we would later experience the terrible vacuum her passing had left. Still, a sense of peace accompanied the necessary sorting out of her possessions. She had been a brave and good wife and mother, and we now entrusted her to the Lord, whom she loved so much during her life.

Her entry into eternity linked me more securely with all of the human race, whether in this life or the next. I sensed myself more connected with all of humanity, more a member of the human race. Death had enlarged my family.

71. Try a Little Trust

Notwithstanding our meditations, death is still that five-letter word we hesitate to pronounce. Our logical minds tell us that Jesus' redemptive death and resurrection should erase fear.

Faith in Jesus' promise assures us that death means not a void, not a vacuum, not an emptiness that awaits us, but rather a meeting with our Redeemer who proved long ago his everlasting love for us.

Certainly one eternal day we will marvel that we ever dreaded what was actually a genuine homecoming—something far more wonderful than the "resting in peace" for which we often pray.

The God who made us knows and loves us well. If we are slow learners about this mysterious matter of death, it matters not—so long as we depend on God in the end.

The simple short prayer, "God, I place all of my trust in you," fits any occasion in our lives. Perhaps it can help erase any remaining fear we have of that moment of welcome into eternity.

72. Thoughts While Waiting for Eternity

Light and darkness play within my life—
starlight and sunlight
moonlight and dusk glow
shadows and darkness
blackness of night.
Every shade from white to gray to black
Nestles within the folds of my life.

Welcome, gladness!
Welcome, sadness!
You are my children,
Dear to me because you are mine.
I claim you: you are mine.

PART ELEVEN

Probing Life's Mystery

At this moment I am reading, seeing, breathing. I am a person endowed with many gifts, and crowning them all is my free will. I have the capacity to spend my moments as I will. I can love and be loved, or I can reject love. I have life and the promise of eternal life. What a mystery life is!

73. Life: Unsolicited Gift

Life is a mystery. We can discern when human life is present and when it is not, but it still remains a mystery.

We receive life as a gift. We have nothing to say about our being chosen to exist as human beings. We have no choice about our time in history, our race, our parentage, our health at birth, our intelligence, our body type, or other personal endowments.

By the time we become aware of such facts about ourselves, we have already been shaped both by our inherited panoply of characteristics and by circumstances associated with our unchosen environment. Like it or not, we have the gift of life, together with certain endowments and opportunities, frailties and limitations.

The mystery of life does not lessen with the years, but increases as we experience more of it. But a few things about life become clearer. It begins in time and continues into eternity. Once begun, it will never end. Life for us human beings stands midway in the created order—half immersed in the spirit world and half immersed in the world of animal, plant, and inanimate creatures.

God must have smiled when he created such a being!

74. Change Means Maturation

Psychological studies as well as our own experiences have defined certain objectives appropriate to each level of human development. We say a child is "behind schedule" if she is not yet walking or talking soon after sixteen months. We expect in most children a beginning sense of the difference between right and wrong by the age of six or so. We are surprised when a post-teen has no desire for independence from home and parents.

Our ability to evaluate appropriate behavior implicitly suggests that physical development should be accompanied by certain intellectual, psychological, social, and emotional changes.

Ideally, the objectives of the various stages of human life in some way move us toward the final goal of life itself, however we interpret it.

Sometimes, though, we do not see that final goal clearly. Even when we have a clear vision of it, we do not find it easy to select the right immediate goals. Life is complex and sometimes even inscrutable, and the way is not always clear. Inexperience, shortsightedness, and impetuosity can lead to unwise choices.

Indeed, we then are grateful for the gift of time and for the ability to change. Still, the gap between aspiration and achievement mystifies us, and at times also depresses us. Fortunately, we retired people have time to make up for lost opportunities.

75. Living in Two Worlds

We strive for an eternal goal, yet achieve now only temporal—temporary—ones. We have spiritual aspirations, yet are limited by time and events not entirely of our choosing. We are called to love as we are loved, yet find ourselves limited in the capacity to love. We are summoned to greatness, yet experience weakness and limitations.

We yearn for wholeness, but find ourselves fragmented. We seek perfection, but see ourselves flawed. We seek truth, but find the quest tedious. We long for rest, but are called to labor. We aspire to our final goal, yet find ourselves ever on the way.

Our physical being is limited by time, place, and circumstances, while our spirit is free to desire, to hope, to long for, to aspire to, and even to reach heights and breadths that far exceed physical possibility.

Life truly is a mystery, even a puzzle. How comforting that the One who made us understands the challenges we face better than we do.

76. Something More, Something Beyond

If even the good times in life can leave us with a sense of incompleteness and frustration, should we not consider the possibility of reaching a wholeness greater than we have known?

The vastness, beauty, and power of the universe hint that there is something more than we now experience. That breath of life breathed into us has set up a dynamism that challenges us to something beyond our unaided capacity. We feel our limitations; still, the creator-creature relationship encourages us to strive to move beyond present limits.

The I in myself is challenged and called forth by the Thou in the creator. This totally Other allows me to know who I am. God reveals self through nature, through the prophetic word, through Sacred Scripture—and especially through the account of the life of his faithful witness, Jesus. Something—Someone?—within us keeps calling us to an existence where limitations will yield to a unity and completeness beyond our present imagining. Otherwise, why would we have a capacity for a happiness that is yet beyond our reach?

There are many reasons why human life remains a mystery to us even as we live it. One is that the world beyond is somewhat alien to us, for we ordinarily acquire our knowledge from sense perception. In the realm of the spirit, we must make room for the Spirit left us by Jesus to continue showing us the way.

77. God's Fidelity

Before a definitive breaking into human history through Jesus, God prepared humankind for incarnated divinity by providing prophetic glimpses. God's desire to seal a covenant with us is clear in both the Old and the New Testaments. Around the year 167 B.C., the prophet Daniel has a vision of a mysterious figure, "one like a son of man" (Daniel 7:13). In the early second century after the coming of Christ, the author of Revelation (14:14) has a vision in which he sees "one like a son of man." The martyr Stephen, even while being stoned to death, sees heaven open and "the Son of Man standing at the right hand of God" (Acts 7:56).

Around 756 B.C., the author of the Songs of the Suffering Servant (Isaiah 42:1–9; 49:1–6; 50:4–11; 52:13–15; 53:2–12) writes of a mysterious figure who suffers for the sins of others. New Testament writers see this mysterious figure as Jesus, who bore our iniquities (Matthew 3:17; Luke 4:17–21; Acts 3:13; 8:32–33). Jesus speaks of himself as "the Son of Man" who is destined to suffer (Mark 8:31; Luke 6:5; 9:58).

These biblical references cover hundreds of years, yet they all point to one reality: that Jesus, the Son of Man, suffered in his human nature to atone for our sins.

With our myopic vision of supernatural realities, we perceive only partially and darkly the great things that God is continually doing in our world, in human history, indeed in us. We are immersed in a wonderful mystery and yet cannot comprehend it.

78. Probing Mysteries of Nature

Out there
we have discovered a star,
a gaseous 2000-degree Fahrenheit mass of glowing
matter.
Oh, the vastness,
the emptiness out there,
seventy-one thousand light years away,
yet our instruments prove it is there.
Scary,
this vastness, this silent immensity:
cold, cruel, distant, inhuman.
I feel enveloped in its emptiness, its speechless
nothingness.
And yet
into this awesome abyss
I throw myself or am thrown,
knowing that the Maker of it all
is nearer to me than I am.
This universe
does not impress its Creator;
it is but a toy to the maker.
"Come," I hear God say,
"My creation is for you to enjoy."

PART TWELVE

Mary,
Post-Resurrection Woman:
Patroness of the Elderly

In temporal affairs, we often call on a sort of negotiator to settle our differences with another. We hire an attorney to negotiate a property dispute. We ask a mutual friend to sound out a third party about a possible reconciliation after a rupture in a friendship. In our dealings with God, we sometimes wish for a go-between who would act as a patron on our behalf. Mary, chosen to mother God's incarnated Son, qualifies as an expert for this role.

79. Mary, Qualified Patroness

A patroness should be someone who has drunk so deeply at the wellsprings of human experience that no joy or sorrow is foreign to her. Each of us wants someone who has sounded the depths of the human heart and can therefore understand what it means to be human: surrounded with temporalities, yet called to a supernatural destiny.

We want someone who can empathize with us in our weaknesses, console us in our sorrows, rejoice with us in our triumphs, someone who has experienced all of human life and who, through God's grace, has matured into the kind of person we can admire and emulate.

Who could be better qualified than Mary, humanity's "solitary boast"? What better intermediary with God than one who shared our nature and who was selected to mother the One sent by God?

Tradition has long given this intercessory role to Mary. Throughout the Christian era, pictorial art and music and literature have reflected a pervasive veneration of the one selected for the role of Jesus' mother.

There is solid scriptural basis for appealing to Mary as our patroness. As Mary stood near the cross, she received from Jesus the commission that would seal her relationship with his disciples (John 19:25–27). Jesus committed his mother to the care of John, who was the stand-in at Calvary for all who love her son. More relevant for us later disciples, Jesus then asked Mary to be mother to John.

80. Misunderstood Prophet

The pilgrimage from Galilee to Jerusalem was Jesus' last. We know of this journey from Mark (15:41) that some of the witnesses of Jesus' crucifixion were "women who had come up to Jerusalem with him." We know Mary was among them, standing by his cross.

During Jesus' ministry we get an occasional glimpse of his mother. After he had been in various regions casting out demons, curing people, and raising others to life, he returned to his own country with his disciples. On the sabbath, Jesus began to teach in the synagogue "in a way that kept his large audience amazed" (Mark 6:2).

His fellow citizens did not see anything in Jesus beyond what they knew of him; he was simply "the carpenter, the son of Mary. . ." (Mark 6:3). They asked: "Where did he get all this? What kind of wisdom is he endowed with?" (Mark 6:2) And, as Mark says (6:3-6), "They found him too much for them. . . . He could work no miracles there . . . so much did their lack of faith distress him."

Mary's suffering must have been intense as she saw Jesus so little understood and his message rebuffed.

Parents and grandparents can easily empathize with Mary as she endured such incidents. In turn, her experiences validate her for her role of patroness who understands our needs.

81. Sorrow and Joy

On one occasion when Jesus' relatives accompanied him to protest the hostility shown him, Mary was among them. They sent in word for Jesus to come out to them: "Your mother and brothers and sisters are outside asking for you" (Mark 3:31–33).

Without denying Mary's role as his mother, Jesus' response indicates that her maternal role extends even to those whom Jesus is now treating as brothers and sisters. "These are my mother and brothers. Whoever does the will of God is brother and sister and mother to me" (Mark 3:34–35).

Her son's claiming a larger world than their simple home must have caused Mary a heart-wrenching that any parent who has suffered the "letting go" of an adult child would recognize.

On Calvary, Jesus formalized Mary's role as spiritual mother of humanity (John 19:25–27):

"Near the cross there stood his mother, his mother's sister, Mary wife of Cleopas, and Mary Magdalen. Seeing his mother there with the disciple whom he loved, Jesus said to his mother, 'Woman, there is your son.' In turn he said to the disciple, 'There is your mother.' From that hour onward, the disciple took her into his care."

The gospel shows us that Mary's life was a medley of the joyful and the sorrowful, the divine and the human, the ordinary and the baffling. No plea of ours will be unfamiliar to her.

82. Mary in Retirement

One can only guess the intensity of Mary's suffering as Jesus endured capture, trials, agony of soul and body, and then condemnation to death by crucifixion. Standing beside her son as he hung on the cross, she could offer no solace except that of her presence, her fidelity.

Mary clearly endured the training and testing that would ready her, in addition to her role as mother of Jesus, for the role also of mother of humanity-redeemed.

Amazed and consoled by Jesus' resurrection, Mary must have puzzled anew at the mystery of her life. After Jesus' ascension, she and the others are found in the upper room devoting themselves to constant prayer. Without doubt, she was a support to those who followed the new way Jesus had taught his followers.

This post-resurrection Mary should be thought of as the patroness of the elderly. Think of Mary in her later years, mellowed in wisdom, understanding so much that was mystery before, filled with loving mercy learned directly from Jesus.

Think of her as totally attentive to those visiting her, perhaps to seek her advice or comfort. See her giving herself peacefully and wholly to the task of each moment, knowing that this is what is demanded of her.

Think of her as the prototype of an ideal retired person.

83. Mother for All Seasons

Released by her death from the restrictions of time and place, Mary now can be present whenever and wherever she wishes. Her spiritual presence is always available to us. She is certainly aware of our human condition, understanding it more clearly than we do. In her we have a patroness who can respond whenever we call on her.

My view of Mary has come a long way from thinking of her as a "lovely lady dressed in blue," hands folded and eyes turned heavenward—a pastel statue that spoke of purity and spring mornings. However, that mental picture inspired me throughout childhood and into my high school years, often giving me courage to hold to ideals I was being taught.

The study of the liturgical year during my teens began maturing my understanding of Mary's pivotal role in salvation history. She was no longer a lifeless, beautiful statue, but an important part of liturgical life and therefore of my spiritual life.

Today I relate to Mary as Mother of Compassion. In a world torn by injustice, violence, poverty, racism, anger, irreverence, and even despair, I can open to Mary the wounds of our society—and my own wounds.

Michelangelo's Pietà presents Mary as the sorrowful, compassionate mother holding the broken, crucified body of Jesus. This evocation of Mary's participation in the passion and death of Jesus epitomizes her claim to be our patroness, for the precious body she holds symbolizes the bruised humanity that her son redeemed and committed to her maternal love.

84. Lady Mary, You I Hail

Lady, queen, celestial mistress,
At whose feet Earth revolves,
For whose delight the planets swing,
Whose bidding sends angels afar,
Whose heart, effulgent Lily, resplendent Rose,
Is upturned to the Trinity?

Beauteous one who are God's delight,
What can I find to interest you in me?
What parallel is there between you and me?
What right or need impels you to me?

Never in me can the answer be found
But in your Son who honored you.
Compassionate Lady, sorrow's Queen,
You saw and shared the Redeemer's life;
You knew and willed the price he paid.
Compassionate Mother, I hail you!

PART THIRTEEN

Walking in Hope and Trust

Whether agile or slowed down, we still are on a journey
and have not finished the course. In many ways, the best
may be yet to come, for we have the time and the
opportunity to concentrate on what truly matters. And
we have the blessed chance to invite as our daily companion on the journey the One who is the way, the truth,
and the life.

85. Walking With Purpose

Each of us elderly has taken many steps since our first faltering ones, and we are still walking. Our physical walking may be as shaky now as were our first tottering steps, or it may still be firm and steady—ready for hiking, skiing, and swimming.

For some, however, physical walking may have become an impossibility because of weakness, a stroke, or amputation.

There are other kinds of "walking," though, that are open to everyone. The intellect seeks truth. The imagination calls forth new possibilities. The human heart opens to love. The spirit speaks in prayer. In fact, these kinds of "walking" can outdistance our legs.

Eventually, for all of us, all kinds of walking reach a point of termination. At some point, neither muscle nor mind responds as it had before.

Yet, joy in living is not nearing an end, but rather a new beginning. In the life beyond death, a person no longer needs to move from here to there, from the unknown to the known, from the present into the future. Life after death is an ever-present Now. The whole of reality will then exist in the Now. There is nothing further toward which the human will and intellect yearn. This life will have found its fulfillment.

Such a prospect holds out a promise of eternal joy.

86. Fathoming the Unknown

The prospect of passing from the life we know to the unknown can be sobering and even frightening. Not knowing makes death seem like something to fear.

Scripture offers images that help us imagine the cessation of life. In one image, life's termination is the weaver severing the last thread on the completed garment (Isaiah 38:12).

We find Jesus speaking of death as sleep: "Our beloved Lazarus has fallen asleep, but I am going there to wake him" (John 11:11). Again, when friends mourn the death of Jairus's daughter, Jesus asks, "Why do you make this din with your wailing? The child is not dead. She is asleep" (Mark 5:39). In these instances, Jesus indicates that physical death is not a permanent condition, but only a stage of life. As we try to envision our own death, we can take hope from Jesus' resurrection from death.

When Jesus drove the money changers from the temple, some people asked for a sign that authorized Jesus to act in that way. He replied, "Destroy this temple, and in three days I will raise it up" (John 2:19).

He was talking about the temple of his body. John adds (2:21–22): "Only after Jesus had been raised from the dead did his disciples recall that he had said this, and come to believe the Scripture and the word he had spoken." This insight reinforced the disciples' belief in Jesus' earlier references to the kingdom beyond. It can also assist us to have faith that death is not the end for us either.

87. A Matter of Choice

The evangelists' records of Jesus' death and resurrection bring into focus the reality that Jesus had come to convey: There is eternal life, open to us after our earthly sojourn; yet each of us is free to choose it or to reject it.

"When the Son of Man comes in his glory, escorted by the angels of heaven, he will sit upon his royal throne, and all the nations will be assembled before him. Then he will separate them into two groups, as a shepherd separates sheep from goats. The sheep he will place on his right: 'Come. You have my Father's blessing! Inherit the kingdom prepared for you'" (Matthew 25:31–35).

He then lists the acts that entitle one to be called "blessed." By such actions our discipleship is tested; it is our following of the one who came to be our Way:

"For I was hungry and you gave me food, I was thirsty and you gave me drink. I was a stranger and you welcomed me, naked and you clothed me. I was ill and you comforted me" (Matthew 25:35–36).

When the just ask when it was that they had done these kind deeds, the story's king gives a response that confirms the idea of our unity with Christ: "I assure you, as often as you did it for one of my least brothers, you did it for me" (Matthew 25:40).

As for those who had neglected to minister in these ways to their neighbors, Jesus declares: "These will go off to eternal punishment, and the just to eternal life" (Matthew 25:46).

For those trying to follow the path Jesus pointed out, his words promise a heavenly home.

88. Reinforcing the Promise

We do not have to look far in the New Testament for words of promise that death is but a passage from one kind of life to another. To Martha, grieving over the death of her brother, Jesus makes a promise meant also for us: "I am the resurrection and the life. If anyone believes in me, even though he dies he will live, and whoever lives and believes in me will never die" (John 11:25–26).

When speaking of himself as the Good Shepherd, Jesus emphasizes his role as a leader whose way we are to follow: "I am the gate. Whoever enters through me will be safe. I came that they might have life and have it to the full" (John 10:9–10).

In his last gathering with his apostles, Jesus once again identifies himself as "the way" and affirms his role as our intermediary: "I am the way, and the truth, and the life; no one comes to the Father but through me" (John 14:6).

We treasure these encouraging promises, for life can be long and difficult. Knowing that there is light at the end of the tunnel makes the walking easier. When we envision the loving welcome awaiting us, anxiety and fear disappear.

89. A Sense of the Future

The experience of many who have preceded us suggests that often people close to death sense that the end is near. Our bodies have a language all their own to inform us of our physical state, sometimes before a doctor can. Such premonitions deepen our seriousness about life's meaning and purpose. These thoughts need not sadden us, but they do lead to serious reflection.

I remember well my visits to my father a few months before his death. His customary intense interest in everything had disappeared, and I would find him sitting quietly and peacefully. After greeting him and inquiring about his health, I would ask what I might do for him.

He would say, "Nothing. I was just thinking." I have found such pensiveness common among the elderly.

They have walked their course and are now, as it were, reviewing that course. They are drawing together the threads of the pattern they have been weaving, in anticipation of the Master's severing of the last thread of life on Earth. They are curious about the home that will be theirs at that time. Wisely, they are reflecting on the joys and wonders of this life in anticipation of those ahead that will outlast and outshine them all. "Eye has not seen, ear has not heard . . ." (1 Corinthians 2:9).

90. Looking Ahead Trustfully

Fortunate are those able to savor the words of comfort and promise Jesus spoke shortly before facing his agony and death:

"Do not let your hearts be troubled. Have faith in God and faith in me. In my Father's house there are many dwelling places; otherwise, how could I have told you that I was going to prepare a place for you? I am indeed going to prepare a place for you, and then I shall come back to take you with me, that where I am you also may be. You know the way that leads where I go" (John 14:1–4).

We elderly can walk in hope and trust, with eyes of faith fixed on those footprints that have led the way till now. Jesus has said "I am the way," and we have followed. He has said "I am the truth," and we have believed. He has said "I am the life," and we walk hopefully toward that life with him which will be eternal.

Whether our physical steps are firm or faltering, the walk homeward is open to all. Saint Irenaeus's motto can spur us to live fully as we near this journey's end: "The glory of God is a person fully alive."

Life on Earth has been and is so beautiful that we cannot imagine the wonders of the hereafter—but if we appreciate the gift of life now, we should be in practice for a glorious eternity.

91. Lessons From a Dewdrop

(To me, the dewdrop is a message from its Maker
about the variety of experiences that must make up any
worthwhile life. Such reflections are part of my attempt
to be, as St. Irenaeus urges, "a person fully alive"—near
ninety—and thereby one who gives glory to God.)

Drawn from the depths of the seven seas,
Snatched from the ocean wave,
Sipped from flowering leas,
Lapped from a distant cave;

Spun by the wind in heaven's blue,
Pierced by the sun's pure ray,
Dropped on a rose at evening dew
Under the stars' milky way;

Wooed by the flowers of summer and fall,
Imbibed by buzzing bee,
Plaything of nature, essence of all:
Whisper your secrets to me.

Tell of the wind in its world-wide roaming,
Tell of the pine trees tall,
Tell of the eagle, graceful in soaring,
Tell of tall mountains and insects small.

Tell of heights where as snow you have lain,
Tell of the stratus cloud,
Tell of morning mists and rain,
Tell of thunders loud.

Tell of a ray of sunlight clear
Shattered within your walls,
Prisming colors—blue, green, red—
Wherever a sunbeam falls.

I see you there in morning's light
Jeweling the daggered grass,
Reflecting all nature in miniature
Within your rounded glass.

PART FOURTEEN

Epilogue: Then and Now

Reviewing the decades past, I find that life is of a piece. What fascinated me as a child echoes in today's interests and dreams and meditations. My hope and my prayer is that my life be realizing today the plan my Maker intended for me as childhood and youth and middle age have given way to advanced years.

92. Who Do Others Say I Am?

Like my own father and many other elderly people I have known, I find myself doing much more serious thinking than I recall doing in my more active years. Some reflections take me back to earlier years when I pondered my identity. Who or what was behind those eyes I viewed in the mirror?

In my own unanswered question lay the seeds of a lifelong search for the meaning of life. Eyes have always fascinated me, because they only partially mask the inner core of a person. Although people do not readily open their souls to others, they unconsciously reveal much about themselves to those who wish to understand. Eyes often register the emotions: fear, hope, anger, love, defiance, sadness.

Posture and gestures can tell us how people perceive themselves. Exchanges in conversation uncover a person's values and attitudes—even a philosophy of life. Intentionally or not, each person I have ever met has revealed at least partially the world within.

And I? What have I imparted to others as our eyes met? I have also revealed much of my inner world, my philosophy of life, my perception of reality, my identity.

As I ponder some of those meetings, I wonder what others discovered about me. What impression did I give?

I hope they saw in me hope, trust, and love; that sometimes at least I let the God-presence within flavor my moments with them.

---

93. Traces of God's Goodness

I wonder how my gaze has changed since the days of
my curious peering into the mirror at the age of four or
five to find out who lived behind those eyes. During the
ensuing years, has my gaze turned more often to others
than to myself? Have I seen more honestly, more wisely?
Has my countenance changed when I encountered someone who did not share my views or who thwarted my
selfish interests? Or have I learned to accept differences?
Have I been able to see the goodness in others despite
our differences? Have I become humble enough to love?

By God's grace, I have acquired some degree of wisdom. I have changed: I have begun to love, have begun
to see the inner core of reality, have begun to perceive
the goodness in each person.

God, who is the ground of all reality, leaves traces of
self in all of creation. I have learned to seek out the traces of goodness through which God reveals the divine
presence, and I have found that everyone and everything, at least in the very fact of its existence, is good. In
rare cases, the trace of goodness may be so hidden that it
is almost invisible; yet with the eyes of faith, one can discover it and can love what is found.

I ask myself what response I make to the goodness
that I discover in people and in things. Perhaps it is
principally in this area that I can claim to have grown in
wisdom, but I see this ideal as an ongoing and pro-
gressive quest that must continue to engage me. The
progress is slow, but I am grateful for each movement
forward in the path of wisdom and love.

94. Lifelong Tutor

The years have been my tutor. As an elderly person, my task is to contemplate the goodness inherent in the years I have lived and to value the lessons learned from others whose life-paths have crossed mine.

When my eyes are closed in death, I hope I will perceive clearly the realities that I have seen only darkly in life. Here I have seen traces of goodness; then I hope to be grasped totally by God. I hope my innocent childhood gaze that sensed something special in myself will then know completely the wonders within that I could get only a glimmer of in this life.

I hope I will have reached spiritual maturity capable of grasping the meaning of suffering. Our task is to learn the wisdom of the mystery of the cross. The challenges we have met in life have been occasions for learning this wisdom. Each challenge has been an opportunity for taking another step toward spiritual maturity.

St. Paul directed a message to the spiritually mature. I can only hope and pray that his words in some ways fit me: "There is, to be sure, a certain wisdom which we express among the spiritually mature. It is God's wisdom: mysterious and hidden. God planned it before all ages for our glory. None of the rulers of this age knew the mystery; if they had, they would never have crucified the Lord of glory. Of this wisdom it is written: 'Eye has not seen, ear has not heard, nor has it so much as dawned on people, what God has prepared for those who love him'" (1 Corinthians 2:6–9).

95. Parting Word

Dare to step into the future,
Dare to be the one you are,
Dare to trust someone
(You will find the Other),
Dare to love and to be loved,
Dare life and discover eternity.

Reflections On My Life

Reflections On My Life

Reflections On My Life

Of Related Interest...

Aging With Joy
Ruth Morrison and Dawn Radtke
Here are practical, workable and effective ways to take charge of
the aging years. For anyone 50+, for children of aging parents
and for anyone who cares for the aging.

ISBN: 0-89622-360-4, 112 pp, $5.95

Letting Go
Reflections and Prayers for Midlife
Judy Esway
These personal meditations and vignettes encourage readers to
face middle age "gracefully and with joy."

ISBN: 0-89622-434-1, 80 pp, $5.95

Stations of the Cross for Older Adults
John van Bemmel
Reflections on the suffering of Jesus related to the process of
aging. A great gift book for older adults.

ISBN: 0-89622-420-1, 32 pp, $1.95

A Way of the Cross for Infirm Women
The Journey to Death & Resurrection
Paulette Ducharme
A sensitive look at the passion of Jesus through the eyes of an
elderly infirm woman.

ISBN: 0-89622-422-8, 32 pp, $1.95

Available at religious bookstores or from

TWENTY-THIRD PUBLICATIONS
P.O. Box 180 • Mystic, CT 06355

1-800-321-0411

Reflections On My Life